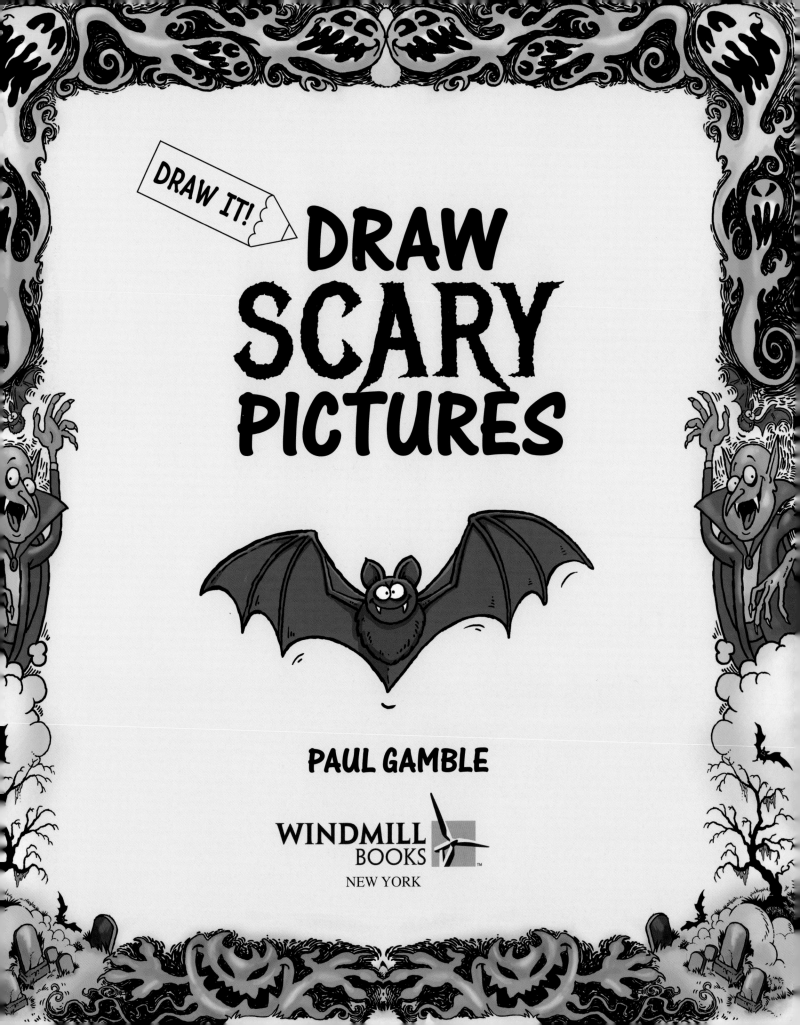

DRAW IT!

DRAW SCARY PICTURES

PAUL GAMBLE

WINDMILL BOOKS
NEW YORK

Published in 2015 by Windmill Books, An Imprint of Rosen Publishing
29 East 21st Street, New York, NY 10010

First Edition

Text: Paul Gamble and Anna Brett

Illustrations: Paul Gamble

Design: Notion Design

Editors: Joe Harris, Anna Brett, and Samantha Hilton

With thanks to Frances Evans and Jessica Williams

Library of Congress Cataloging-in-Publication Data

Gamble, Paul, 1958-

 Draw scary pictures / By Paul Gamble. -- First Edition.

    pages cm. -- (Draw it!)

Includes index.

ISBN 978-1-4777-9148-6 (library binding) -- ISBN 978-1-4777-9149-3
(pbk.) -- ISBN 978-1-4777-9150-9 (6-pack)

1. Characters and characteristics in art--Juvenile literature.
2. Drawing--Technique--Juvenile literature. I. Title.

NC825.C43G367 2015

741.2--dc23

                         2014008370

Printed in the United States

SL004213US

CPSIA Compliance Information: Batch #AS4102WM: For Further Information contact Windmill Books, New York, New York at 1-866-478-0556

CONTENTS

GETTING STARTED

This book will teach you how to draw a cast of wonderful characters. Simply follow the step-by-step instructions and get drawing!

1. Start with a plain piece of unlined paper. If you are going to paint your picture, you should use thick paper.

2. Use a pencil to copy the step-by-step instructions. Soft pencils are good for rough sketches. Hard pencils are best for details.

3. Draw over your pencil guide lines with a black pen or a thin brush and black ink. The ink must be waterproof if you are going to add watercolor paints to your picture.

4. When the pen ink has dried, use a large, soft eraser to remove the rough pencil marks. Now your picture is looking nice and neat!

5. Complete your picture by coloring it in with colored felt-tip pens, pencils, or paint.

6. Paintbrushes come in different shapes. When painting, use a thin, pointed brush for detail and a fatter brush for flat areas of color.

GOO MONSTER

1. To create Goo Monster's shape, draw three squashed circles overlapping each other.

2. Start his horrible face with eyeballs and a large mouth. Add lines and ovals for his arms.

3. Use the eyebrows to make him look mean. Make his arms look big and strong, and add hands, too.

4. Draw in his deadly slime bucket and the fingers on his left hand. Add pupils to his savage stare!

5. Finish drawing the bucket and his hands. Now let's add some slime!

6. Fill in his mouth and eyes, then go slime crazy! Make him as gloopy and horrible as you can! Finally, color him green, and make his bucket brown.

SPACE SQUID

1. To start Space Squid, you need to draw two egg-shaped ovals overlapping each other, one large and one small.

2. Draw circles for his eyes in the smaller oval and a wobbly line for his mouth in the larger oval.

3. Pencil in the top of his mouth and the guide line across his eyes where his brow will be. Then add two swirly lines for his tentacles.

4. Space Squid has four tentacles. You can doodle any shape or swirl to start them.

5. Finish the tentacles. Give him pupils and teeth, then mark where his school tie will be.

6. Shade in his mouth, and don't forget to add the shreds of material caught on his teeth. He's just taken a bite out of something!

EGYPTIAN MUMMY

1. Start Egyptian Mummy by drawing a large circle and then adding a small rectangle for his body.

2. Draw two small circles where the hands will be and then two ovals for the feet.

3. Sketch in his arms and Egyptian Mummy begins to take shape. You can add the open mouth now, too.

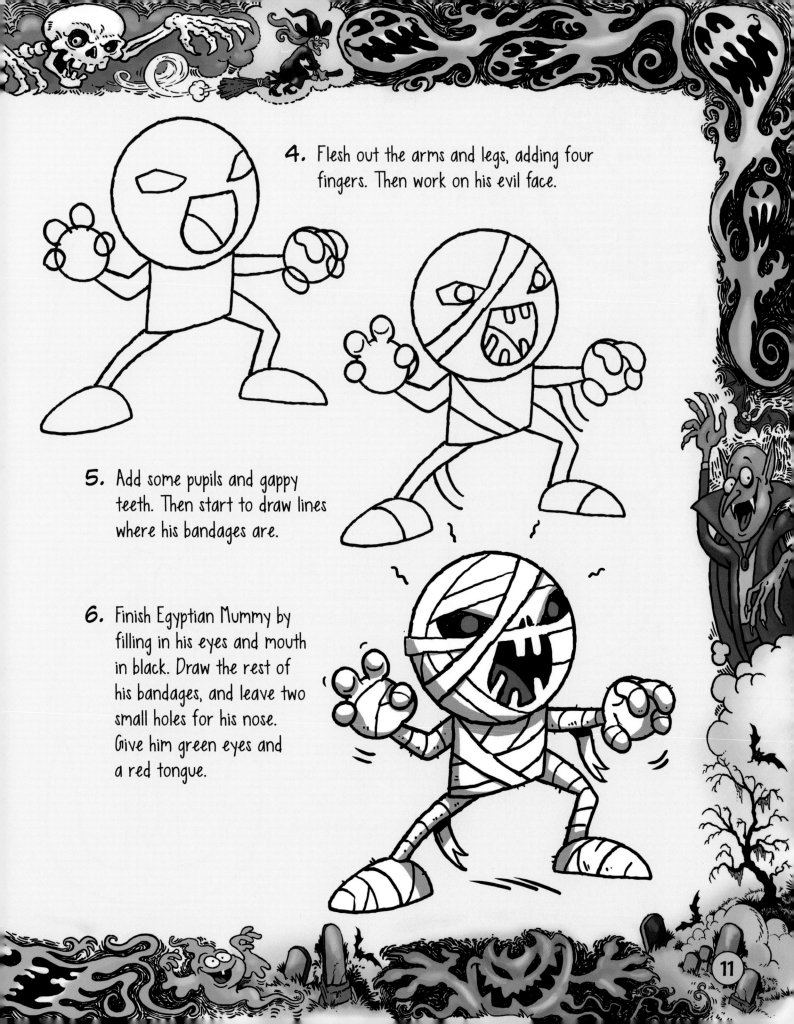

4. Flesh out the arms and legs, adding four fingers. Then work on his evil face.

5. Add some pupils and gappy teeth. Then start to draw lines where his bandages are.

6. Finish Egyptian Mummy by filling in his eyes and mouth in black. Draw the rest of his bandages, and leave two small holes for his nose. Give him green eyes and a red tongue.

PHARAOH

1. Begin by drawing two curved shapes for this fearsome Pharaoh's headdress and neck plate.

2. Next, add a curve where the Pharaoh's head is going to be and two shapes to mark the bottom of the headdress.

3. Draw a curved guide line to mark the top of his head, and put in the outline of the snake on his crown. You can also draw in his long beard.

4. Add two lines around the bottom of the neck plate, then give the Pharaoh his ears, eyes, and mouth. Add in the sneering snake's eyes and nose.

5. Add the stripes on the headdress, and braid the beard. Give him big eyebrows, eyeliner, fangs, and markings on his cheeks.

6. Add pupils, a furrowed brow, and some shading to finish your majestic portrait. Color it in regal gold and royal blue!

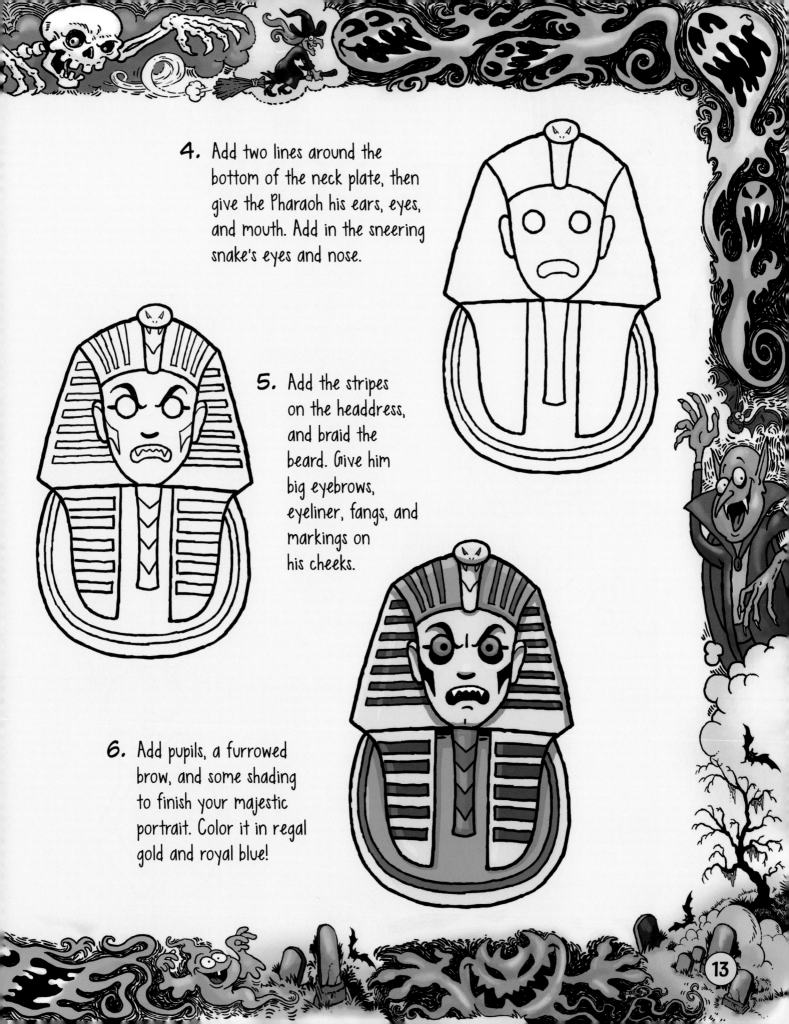

MR. BONES

1. Start Mr. Bones by drawing a semicircle where his head will be, plus two kidney shapes for his ribs and hips.

2. Add in his triangular jaw and bones for the top of his arms and legs. Practice drawing the classic bone shape.

3. Draw in the rest of the arms and legs, paying attention to his pose. Then draw small rectangles where his spine will be.

4. Mr. Bones does not enjoy being dead, so give him angry eyes! Add small shapes for all his joints.

5. Draw pupils and a mouth. Then add fingers, toes, ribs, and splits in his arm and leg bones.

6. Add the finishing touches to Mr. Bones as shown in the picture, and you're done. He's chasing all those pupils who haven't done their history homework!

BOO

1. Boo starts life as a curved rectangle. Easy!

2. His arms are up in the air and shaped like bananas. Spirits don't have legs, so make the bottom of the rectangle ragged.

3. Add circles for hands, a curve at the back of his head, and some more tatters at the bottom.

4. Boo's clawed hands make up for his lack of legs! Now's the time to add a wicked grin.

5. Give him evil eyes by drawing little semicircles. His jagged teeth are just mini triangles.

6. Boo's in fright mode, so add some movement lines around his body. Shade around his eyes and his jagged bottom. He is a creepy shade of green.

WANDA WITCH

1. Begin with a shape like a witch's hat. It's a triangle with a longer bottom.

2. Draw a circle inside the triangle, and add two pointy arms on either side.

3. Draw a circle around her head, a line for the bottom of her dress, and a V shape for the broom.

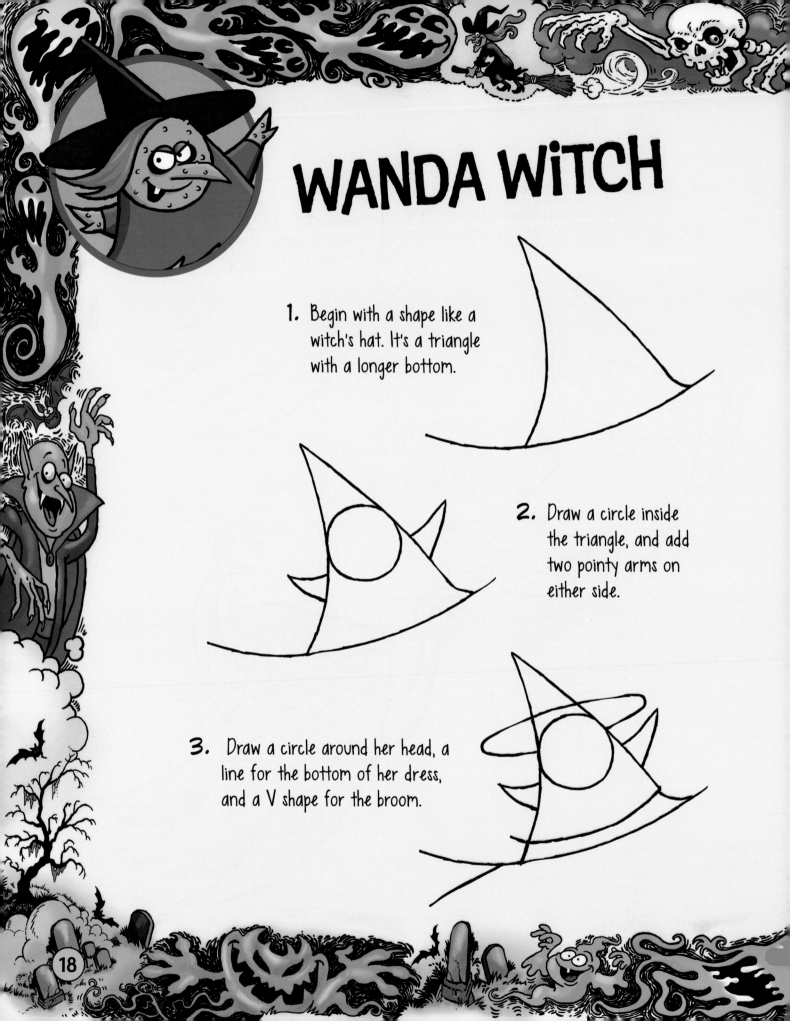

4. Get your eraser out, and suddenly Wanda begins to take shape. Draw in her feet, face, hands, and hair.

5. The tip of her hat is bent, a lot like her large nose! Draw it in, along with her eyelids and open mouth.

6. The finishing touches include lots of warts! She has a single tooth and wicked eyes. Her face and dress are green. Watch her fly into the night to cause mischief!

ZOMBIE ZEKE

1. A bell or a pear? This is how Zeke starts life. You could try to draw a whole zombie army.

2. Add a circle for the head and two ovals for his feet.

3. Draw a triangle between his feet to get the shape of his legs. Two circles will become his hands.

4. Add circles for his eyes, a bean-shaped mouth, tattered pants legs, and zombie arms.

5. I don't think a dentist would be happy with Zeke's teeth, since even his floppy tongue is trying to avoid them!

6. Now add the details: pupils, shadows under his eyes, ragged clothes, and drops of slop!

VAMPIRE BAT

1. Vampire Bat begins life as a large triangle with a semicircle on top.

2. To get the shape of the wings, connect the ends of the semicircle with the edges of the triangle. The little circle will be his head.

3. Erase the top of the triangle, and add lines across the wings. Draw in his body.

4. You can draw in the full wing shape now. Add his pointy ears, too.

5. Time to add a face and erase all the guide lines you no longer need.

6. Finish the wings, and give him a furry body. Last but not least come his fangs. He is a vampire bat, after all! Color him purple.

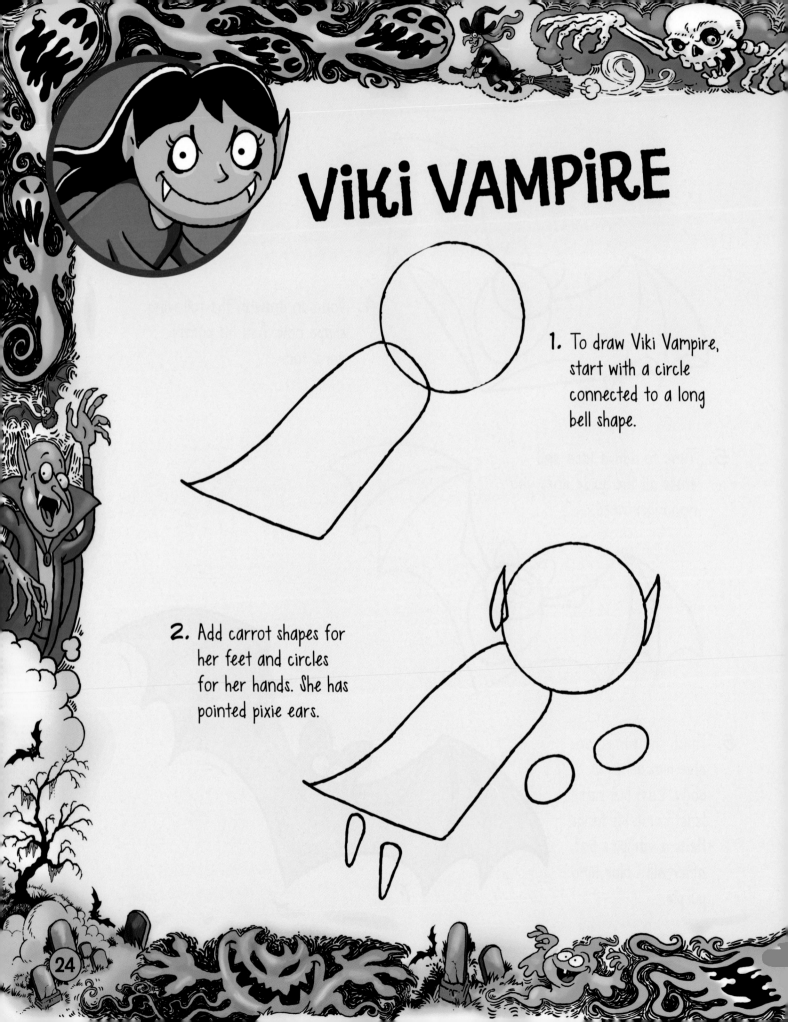

ViKi VAMPiRE

1. To draw Viki Vampire, start with a circle connected to a long bell shape.

2. Add carrot shapes for her feet and circles for her hands. She has pointed pixie ears.

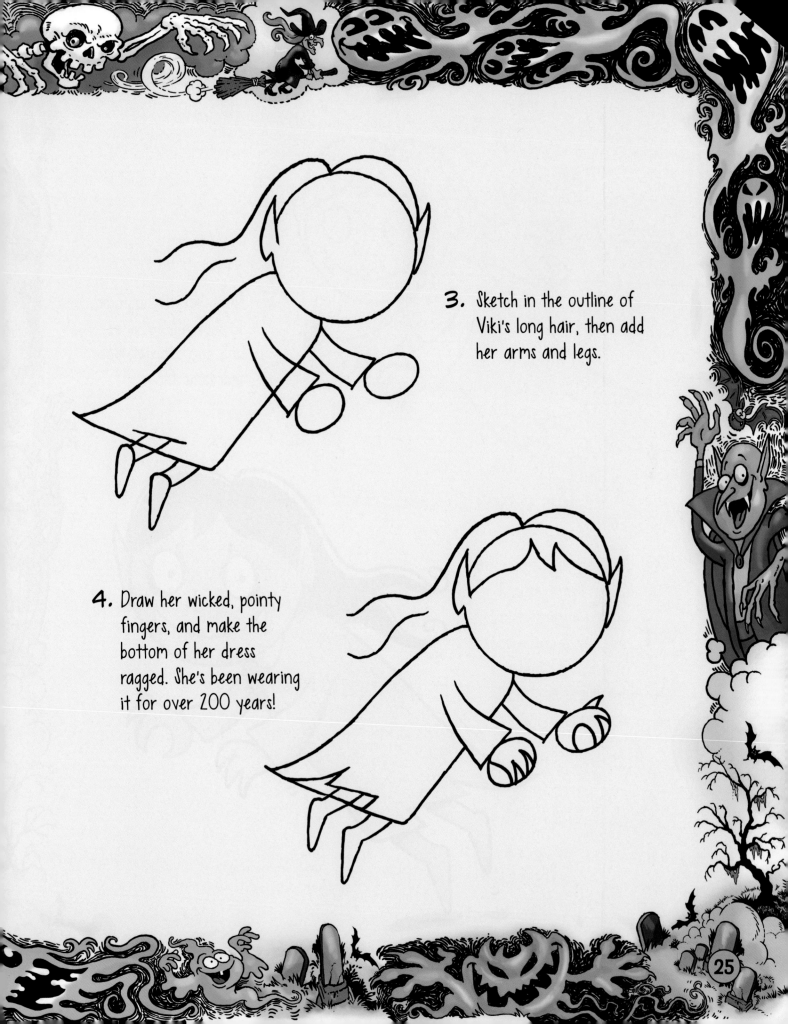

3. Sketch in the outline of Viki's long hair, then add her arms and legs.

4. Draw her wicked, pointy fingers, and make the bottom of her dress ragged. She's been wearing it for over 200 years!

5. Finish her flowing hair to show she's flying, and don't forget those fearsome fangs.

6. Add dark shadows under her eyes and sloping eyebrows to give her a crafty look. Give her a blood-red dress and green skin. Vamp-tastic!

DITZY DRACULA

1. Ditzy Dracula's no square, he's shaped like a rectangle! Add a circle at the top for his head.

2. Draw a triangle for his body and two smaller circles for his hands.

3. Two triangles look like ears, but they're really the top of his cape!

4. Time to add some eyes and give the bottom of the cape a batwing shape.

5. Now draw in his pointy ears and fingers, and add his cheeky face!

6. Finally, add fangs and finishing touches. Color him in with purple, red, and black pencils.

DRAWING A SCARY SCENE

Now that you have learned how to draw all kinds of different scary characters, why not bring some of them together to create a whole scene?

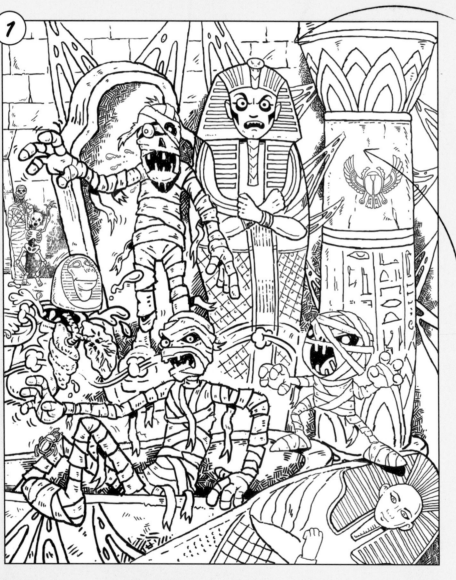

1

First, make a rough sketch of your picture in pencil, using simple shapes. Then add detail. Try to fill the whole space.

Have fun making your background as spooky as possible. We have added a mummy's coffin, an evil-looking Pharaoh, lots of cobwebs, and gooey green slime.

Now it's time to add some color! Think about which shades work well together and how they make you feel.

We chose strong, bright colors for our scary scene. Green and purple look best. You can use bright red for your characters' scary eyes!

We have drawn spooky mummies coming back to life in a scary Egyptian tomb. Position them so that they seem to be coming off the page toward you.

It's a good idea to place your characters in lots of different poses to create a sense of energy and excitement.

GLOSSARY

guide line (GYD LYN) A simple line that shows where to fill in a drawing with more lines or color.

hard pencil (HARD PEN-sul) A pencil with a hard lead that is good for making thin strokes and fine details in a drawing.

movement lines (MOOV-ment LYNZ) Lines that show motion.

rough sketch (RUF SKECH) A drawing made quickly to give an idea of the finished picture.

scene (SEEN) A picture of a place.

semicircle (SE-mee-surh-kul) Half of a circle.

soft pencil (SOFT PEN-sul) A pencil with a soft lead that is good for making thick strokes or filling in a drawing.

FURTHER READING

Emberley, Ed. *Ed Emberley's Drawing Book of Weirdos.* New York: LB Kids, 2005.
Levy, Barbara Soloff. *How to Draw Funny Monsters.* Mineola, NY: Dover Publications, 2009.

WEBSITES

For web resources related to the subject of this book, go to: www.windmillbooks.com/weblinks and select this book's title.

INDEX

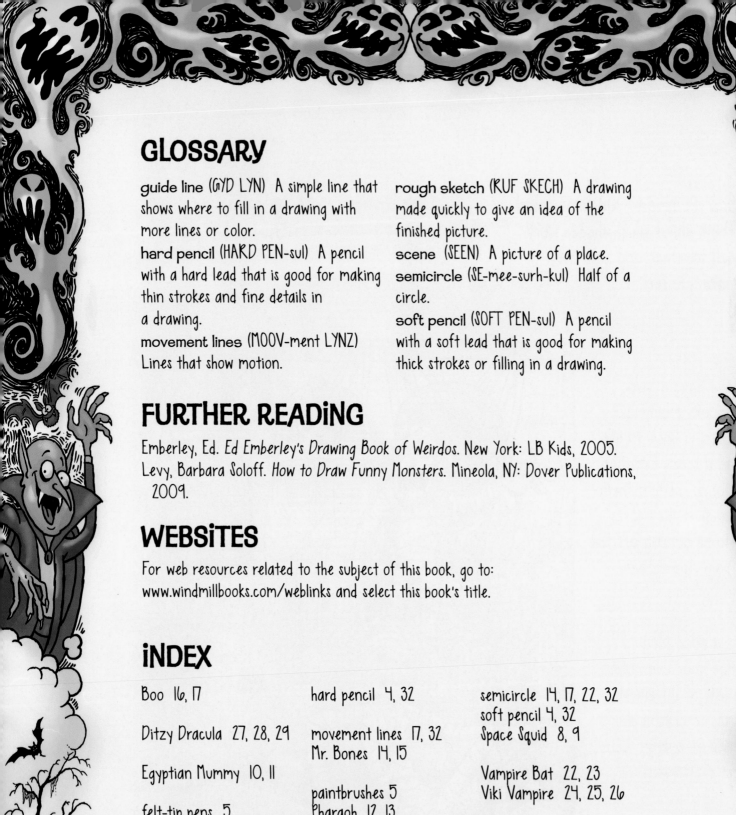